AUSTRALIA TAKE A BOW

First published in 1988 by
John Ferguson Pty Ltd, Publishers
in association with
Angus & Robertson Publishers.

Angus & Robertson Publishers
Unit 4, Eden Park, 31 Waterloo Road
North Ryde, NSW 2113, Australia, and
16 Golden Square, London WIR 4BN
United Kingdom.

John Ferguson Pty Ltd
100 Kippax St
Surry Hills, NSW 2010
Australia

© John Ferguson Pty Ltd in 1988

National Library of Australia
Cataloguing-in-publication entry
Australia take a bow.
ISBN 0 949118 31 1.
1. Australia – Description and travel – 1976 – Views. I.
Morris, Brian.
944.06'3'0222.

Front Cover: Berriwollock, the Mallee, in Victoria
Pages 2 & 3: The Trans Australian railway from
the Stuart Highway in South Australia
Pages 4 & 5: Sunset on the northern New South Wales
coast, near Coffs Harbour
Back Cover: Dirt track, north-east South Australia

Designer: Maree Cunnington
Executive Editor: Karen Eyre
Research Editor: Susan Orr
Picture Editors: Maree Cunnington, Christina de Water
Typesetter: Keyset Phototype
Colour Separations: Dot 'n Line, Australia
Printer: Everbest, Hong Kong

AUSTRALIA TAKE A BOW

THE LIFE, LANDSCAPE AND PEOPLE

BRIAN MORRIS

PHOTOGRAPHS BY
WILDLIGHT PHOTO AGENCY

ANGUS
& ROBERTSON
PUBLISHERS

INTRODUCTION

European settlement of Australia began on 26 January 1788 with the arrival at Port Jackson of the First Fleet under Captain Arthur Phillip. Phillip had been sent to establish a penal colony to cope with the overflow of British prisons, after the War of Independence had prevented Britain from sending its felons to the American colonies. He commanded a convoy of 11 vessels carrying more than 700 convicts and nearly 300 British officers, marines, wives and children. The raising of the British flag at Sydney Cove brought the colony of New South Wales into being 18 years after the discovery of the east coast of Australia by the celebrated British navigator Captain James Cook.

This was, of course, not the beginning of human occupation of Australia. When European settlement began, there were an estimated 750,000 Aborigines living in about 600 tribal communities spread throughout this vast land, their ancestors having been there for some 40,000 years, largely untouched by outside influence. Nomadic hunter-gatherers, the Aborigines lived in harmony with the land and had a complex system of beliefs explaining the creation of the earth, which happened in what they called the Dreamtime.

In the first year of the colony's existence, the new settlers almost perished from famine. But they eventually prospered, as did the other Australian colonies subsequently established: Van Diemen's Land, later renamed Tasmania; then the Settlement at Moreton Bay, which separated from New South Wales to become the colony of Queensland; the Swan River settlement (Western Australia); the Port Phillip district (Victoria); and finally South Australia, the only Australian colony established without the introduction of convicts.

Each colony developed largely independently of the others, which were scattered around a coastline of 36,735 kilometres (22,827 miles). As time passed, they realised the advantages of closer co-operation and, eventually, of unity. In 1901 they joined together into a federation of states and became the Commonwealth of Australia. Today, 87 years after the Federation and 200 years after the inauspicious beginning on the shores of Sydney Cove, Australia is a vibrant country with a population of more than 16 million, a technologically advanced nation with a sophisticated level of artistic and cultural achievement.

AUSTRALIA TAKE A BOW is a tribute to the Australian way of life that has emerged during the past 200 years. The images have been arranged without formal structure, to show contrasting aspects of Australian life and to provide a window on this vast continent, a chance to explore Australia through the camera lenses of four of Australia's best documentary still photographers.

The observations recorded in AUSTRALIA TAKE A BOW complement a series of seven films of the same name made for television by Brian Morris, one of Australia's leading documentary film producers. Shot on location in the six states and two territories, the films are edited to music, using no narration or dialogue. The film series and the book have been sponsored by IBM Australia Limited.

Still photographers Carolyn Johns, Philip Quirk, Oliver Strewe and Grenville Turner accompanied the AUSTRALIA TAKE A BOW film crew on their journeys throughout Australia. Over a period of 18 months they travelled more than 180,000 kilometres. They captured on film the extraordinary contrasts in the Australian landscape, from the tropical rainforests of far northern Queensland to the remote deserts of the centre, from the rugged ochre cliffs in South Australia to the lush green fields of Tasmania, from the alpine country of the Snowy Mountains to the surfing beaches of the east coast, from the sparsely populated outback to the thronging, multicultural cities. Moreover, they photographed the Australian people, at work and at play, celebrating, demonstrating, performing or simply relaxing. They observed and recorded the independent spirit of the people, the qualities that bind together a nation despite the individual differences of the people and the great distances that separate the communities.

Traditionally, Australia's links with Britain have been close because of constitutional ties, a predominantly Anglo-Saxon population and family and cultural associations. Today, however, the constitutional links with Britain have been severed, and four out of ten Australian residents were either born outside Australia, many in Europe or Asia, or have at least one parent who was born overseas. The present cosmopolitan character of the nation is largely the result of the major wave of immigration that began after World War II, which has contributed to the population more than doubling since 1945. The migrant influence on social customs, food, the arts, sport, business and intellectual life has resulted in a new national identity and changes in the Australian way of life.

These changes are most obvious in the capital cities. Melbourne, for example, has more Greeks than in any city outside Greece. There are also more people of Maltese descent living in Australia than there are in Malta itself, and since the first Vietnamese 'boat people' arrived in Darwin in 1976, Australia has accepted probably more Indo-Chinese refugees, in proportion to population, than any other Western country. Out of the cities, while modern technology may have altered the way of doing things, country folk have largely retained the traditional way of life and the easy going attitude associated with the bush.

For many years the prosperity of Australia depended almost exclusively on the export of wool. It was said that Australia rode on the sheep's back. Today wool is still a major export, and rural produce accounts for a significant part of the country's export income. But since the 1960s, minerals — iron ore, coal, bauxite, nickel, uranium, copper, silver-lead-zinc, oil and natural gas, as well as gold and diamonds — have become increasingly important to the Australian economy. Changes have come about for the workers. Nowadays the drover is likely to travel in a well-appointed caravan and truck, and miners in such huge operations as the Argyle diamond mine in the Kimberleys and Mount Newman iron-ore operation in the Hamersley Ranges live in motel-style villages and can relax after work in the company's swimming pool or on the golf course with its red-earth fairways.

In recent years, Australia has become a regional centre in the Pacific area for service industries such as banking and financial services, education, medicine and, of course, tourism, Australia's fastest-growing industry. North Americans, Japanese and Europeans are coming to Australia in increasing numbers; it is estimated that by the turn of the century Australia will be welcoming five million visitors a year.

While Sydney, with its world-renowned harbour and Opera House and the nearby Blue Mountains, is the essential first stopping-off place for most visitors to Australia, the tourist package may include any of the modern resorts on the coast and the Barrier Reef or in the outback and visits to the more remote and less frequented places in the far north and north-west of the country. In city or country, the attractions are endless. Whether it is watching the Melbourne Cup at Flemington or a rodeo at Mareeba, travelling on the Indian Pacific across the Nullarbor Plain or cruising in a luxury vessel through the Whitsunday Passage, attending a surf carnival at Bondi or the football grand final at the Melbourne Cricket Ground, admiring the grandeur of Ayers Rock or the ingenuity of the dug-out houses at Coober Pedy, watching the birdlife on the Coorong – there is something for everyone to do as well as see. The excitement and spectacle of these activities are also caught on film in the television series AUSTRALIA TAKE A BOW, which has been cut to classical and contemporary music.

Since Captain Phillip founded his penal colony at Port Jackson in 1788, Australia has developed into a competitive nation with a strong identity of its own and a lifestyle that is envied throughout the world. In its Bicentennial Year, the country and its people are proudly portrayed in this permanent and never-to-be repeated colour record.

The following are extracts from speeches given by the Australian Prime Minister, Bob Hawke, and His Royal Highness, The Prince of Wales, at the Bicentennial Australia Day ceremony at the Sydney Opera House on January 26, 1988.

'What is it that links us, in our generation, with the generations which have gone before? It is not only the fact that, for the past 200 years and to this day, we have been a nation of immigrants. It is not only the fact that we share together this vast continent as our homeland. It is not only the shared inheritance of all that has been built and achieved here over the past 200 years. And it is not only the common bond of institutions, standards, language and culture. In today's Australia, our very diversity is an ever-growing source of the richness, vitality and strength of our community . . .

That factor is: a commitment to Australia and to its future. It is that common commitment which binds the Australian-born of the seventh or eighth generation and all those of their fellow Australians born in any of the 130 countries from which our people are drawn.

In Australia, there is no hierarchy of descent; there must be no privilege of origin. The commitment is all . . . our commitment to Australia and Australia's cause – the cause of freedom, fairness, justice and peace.'

R.J.L. Hawke

'Almost every country on earth is the old country to some family in Australia. Coming from your first old country, and celebrating the twenty-second anniversary of my first transportation to Australia, let me say on behalf of all the lands and people who have contributed to your heritage, that you have the best of us.

Australia is its own creation, but in a very real sense it belongs to the world. Australia is an international nation. People from anywhere feel at home here in Australia. It's that sort of place. In two world wars, Australians fought wholeheartedly against intolerance and tyranny. They didn't just fight for the old empire, which has now receded into history. They fought for freedom: which lasts, if it's nurtured.

One of Australia's oldest ties with the oldest of its old countries is the rule of law. They were harsh judges who sent the first Australians out here, but they were wisely framed laws that turned the convicts into free men and women. And free men and women helped make a democracy which has become a model for the world . . .'

H.R.H., The Prince of Wales

(Above) Uluru (Ayers Rock), the world's largest monolith, in the Northern Territory. The rock is almost 350 metres high (1,144 feet) and 8 kilometres (5 miles) around the base.

(Previous page) The remote and ruggedly beautiful shores of Lizard Island, a prime diving and black marlin fishing location, 90 kilometres (56 miles) north of Cooktown between the Queensland coast and the Great Barrier Reef. The island, with its 24 beaches and a huge blue lagoon, attracts diving enthusiasts from all over the world.

(Above) Blossom trees in spring in the Barossa Valley, South Australia. The Barossa Valley is the state's premier wine-growing area, producing many of the country's best wines.

Contract drovers break their journey
on the road in the Hay district of
south-western New South Wales.

19

The bare hills of Queenstown create a weird moonscape effect in the 'wild west' of Tasmania. Queenstown is the site of the Mount Lyell company's copper mine; the barren landscape has resulted from the sulphurous smelting process that was introduced early in the century.

The Renison Mine, near Zeehan, on the west coast of Tasmania, is the largest underground tin mine in the world. During the last century, Zeehan was a major silver-mining area, commonly known as 'the silver city'.

(Above) A Kalgoorlie goldminer emerges smiling from the pit after
a hard day's work. Kalgoorlie, in Western Australia, is Australia's
richest source of gold and one of the world's main goldfields.

(Right) George Walters, 72, a well-known stockhorse breeder
and rider in the Coraki area, in northern New South Wales.

(Right) Waiting for the early morning mist to clear – contract buffalo catchers on an Aboriginal cattle station at Peppimenarti, on the Bangard Plain in the north-west of the Northern Territory. Cattle stations in the Top End frequently cover areas in excess of 8,000 square kilometres (3,000 square miles).

(Overleaf) The Oodnadatta Pink Roadhouse is a bright landmark in the arid region of South Australia, 200 kilometres (120 miles) south of the Northern Territory border. Owned by Lynnie and Adam Plate, the roadhouse provides a map and information service for the Simpson Desert and historic Oodnadatta Track, which links the Flinders Ranges with Ayers Rock.

Early-morning mist veils the power station at Wallerawang, on the western side of the Blue Mountains, 160 kilometres (100 miles) from Sydney. Most of the electricity in New South Wales is supplied by coal-fired power stations on coalfields located to the north, west and south of Sydney.

(Previous page) Wingham Brush, an eight-hectare (20-acre) area of rainforest on the outskirts of Wingham, about 25 kilometres (15 miles) west of Taree in New South Wales. The rainforest is a regular roosting site for fruit bats.

(Above) Mist shrouds an early autumn morning near the Molonglo River in the Australian Capital Territory.

(Right) Passengers prepare for an early morning hot-air balloon flight in the Hunter Valley of New South Wales. The balloons reach heights of up to 606 metres (2,000 feet).

(Above) Country cottages in the quiet rural retreat of Berrima in the Southern Highlands of New South Wales. One of the best remaining examples of a small Australian town of the 1830s, Berrima has a large collection of historic sandstone buildings, including a convict-built jail.

(Above) A suburban house at Dover Heights in Sydney.

(Overleaf) Fire races through a section of Kakadu National Park, near the Arnhem Land escarpment in the Northern Territory, during the close of the dry season in September.

(Above) Morning in the Blue Mountains after an overnight snowfall. The Blue Mountains, which were crossed by the explorers Blaxland, Lawson and Wentworth in 1813, are the next most popular tourist attraction in New South Wales after Sydney, drawing two million visitors a year.

(Left) Medlow Bath railway station in the Blue Mountains of New South Wales awaits visitors to the famous Hydro-Majestic Hotel, located opposite. The name of the station refers to the spa baths of the hotel, which imported its baths water from Germany around the turn of the century.

A rocky outcrop forms a landmark on the Sturt Highway, south of Tennant Creek, in the Northern Territory.

Red gums on the Murray River in Victoria.

(Above) London Bridge, a limestone formation on the Victorian coast in the Port Campbell National Park. The bridge, which is about 40 metres (130 feet) high, forms part of a spectacular coastline that includes the famous 'Twelve Apostles'.

(Left) Australian artist Ross Manwaring sketches the landscape at Lake Eyre, Australia's largest salt lake, in South Australia.

(Above) The Pinnacles cast long afternoon shadows over the surrounding coastal landscape, near Lancelin, north of Perth in Western Australia. The Pinnacles, a unique limestone formation, were a deterrent to early Dutch sailors who from a distance mistook them for natives.

(Right) Reflections in the river at Geikie Gorge National Park, a major tourist attraction in Western Australia. Cruises operate down the river from April to November.

(Above) Sunset on Sunrise Road, Eumundi, inland from Noosa,
north of Brisbane, Queensland.

(Right) A park ranger cruises down the river at Geikie Gorge
National Park in Western Australia. The gorge, which cuts
through an ancient fossilised coral reef, is surrounded by dense
vegetation — home to a variety of wildlife, including the Johnson
River crocodile.

Members of the Bardi Aboriginal community outside the general store at One Arm Point in the north-west of Western Australia. The government-funded settlement provides housing, health services and schooling for 350 members of the Bardi tribe, originally from Sunday Island, 12 kilometres (7½ miles) east of One Arm Point.

53

A church at Mount Wilson in the Blue Mountains, west of Sydney. A number of country retreats were built at Mount Wilson early this century.

(Above) A model-yacht enthusiast in Perth, Western Australia, during the finals of the America's Cup participates in another kind of competition on a different scale.

(Left) A Hamilton Island cruise operator puts in a hard day's work on the Great Barrier Reef in Queensland.

The *Yendys,* a fully restored 18-footer, built about 1924, sails the waters of Sydney Harbour. Owned by the Sydney Maritime Museum, the carvel-built vessel established a club record in 1937 by winning seven events, including three championships.

(Left) A view of Sydney from Lavender Bay, on the north side of the harbour, taking in Luna Park, the Sydney Harbour Bridge and the Sydney Opera House. Completed in 1973, the Sydney Opera House is Australia's premier tourist attraction.

(Right) Sydney harbour, looking west, from the deck of a private charter yacht. Sydney is a paradise for yachtsmen all year round.

A Torres Strait Islander spearfishes in the translucent reef waters at Warrabah Island, also known as Sue Island, off Cape York.

(Left) An islander grapples with a huge reef turtle in the Coral Sea off the tip of the Cape York peninsula in Queensland.

(Below) Islanders from the Cape York township of Bamaga fish for giant turtles in the coral waters of northern Australia.

(Left) Wind surfers gather for a race on Sydney Harbour.

(Below) The Australian flag makes a patriotic statement during the fervour that swept Fremantle in Western Australia during the finals of the 1987 America's Cup challenge. The United States challenger, *Stars and Stripes,* skippered by Dennis Conner, defeated *Kookaburra III* skippered by Iain Murray, 4-0. Australia made sporting history when it wrested the America's Cup from the United States on 26 September, 1983.

(Overleaf) Sydney Harbour, looking east towards the heads, on Australia Day 1988 – the year of the Bicentenary. Governor Arthur Phillip, who arrived with the First Fleet, raised the British flag at Sydney Cove on 26 January 1788.

(Left) A local Torres Strait Islander works on a housing site at Bamaga, on the tip of Cape York Peninsula in Queensland.

(Below) A security officer stands guard at the front gate of the Royal Mint in Perth, Western Australia. The mint, which was established around the turn of the century to convert the product of the Golden Mile into sovereigns and half-sovereigns, is today the home of the Gold Corporation, which produces the Australian Nugget series of gold coins.

An Aboriginal child leans wistfully in the shade at the One Arm Point Aboriginal reserve, Western Australia.

A young member of the Ngadadgara tribe at Warburton
Aboriginal Reserve, located between the Gibson and Great
Victoria deserts in Western Australia.

This unusual patterned brickwork is a feature of the St Peter's
Anglican Rectory in the inner city Sydney suburb of Darlinghurst.
The Victorian Gothic building, which is classified by the
National Trust, was completed in 1872 at a cost of £1,600.

An Aboriginal painting using vibrant acrylic colours on canvas tells a story from the Dreamtime mythology at the Aboriginal Art Centre in Sydney. The painting is by Jeannie Nungarrayi Egan, of the Yuendumu Aboriginal community in the Northern Territory, north-west of Alice Springs.

(Previous page) Boulders on the track in the arid central Australian region of Kulgera in the Northern Territory.

(Below) The Bungle Bungle Range, located 160 kilometres (100 miles) south of Kununurra in the Kimberley region of Western Australia. A popular tourist attraction, the imposing sandstone chasms and peaks of the Bungle Bungles were formed 350 million years ago during the Devonian Age and cover an area of 450 square kilometres (175 square miles).

A retired farmer stands outside a work shed on his sheep property at Gungahlin in the Australian Capital Territory.

(Above) The force behind the wheel — a truck driver at the Argyle diamond mine in Western Australia. The huge trucks can carry up to 75 tonnes of mining debris.

(Right) The lights of the Argyle diamond mine illuminate the night sky in the Kimberley region of Western Australia.

(Overleaf) An extensive vista of ochre cliffs five kilometres (three miles) north of Lyndhurst on the northern tip of the Flinders Ranges in South Australia. A source of ochre for the Aborigines up until the turn of the century, the cliffs display a spectacular range of colours, including reds, browns, yellows and white.

Wild horses roam the O'Donnell Range, about 170 kilometres
(102 miles) south of Kununurra in Western Australia. The horses,
which are used for mustering on cattle stations, are let run wild
during the wet season and broken in again during the dry.

Feral donkeys gather in the Pilbara region, in the north-west corner of Western Australia. The donkeys, which have reached pest proportions, were orginally introduced to carry bales of wool from sheep stations to the seaport of Wyndham.

A wallaby basks in the early morning light in the Blue Mountains, 100 kilometres (60 miles) west of Sydney.

(Previous page) A typical bush scene in the Flinders Ranges in South Australia. The rugged ranges contain examples of Aboriginal art dating back about 10,000 years.

The jewel colours of the Cathedral of Ferns, a forest of tree ferns
at Mount Wilson, west of Sydney. A remote and secluded area,
Mount Wilson is well known for its English-style gardens, many
of which are open to the public in spring and autumn.

The exterior of the indoor swimming hall at the Australian
Institute of Sport in Canberra. The Institute, which opened in
1981, provides first-class coaching and training facilities for the
élite of Australia's athletes.

A 25-metre shaded pool is among the unusually high standard of facilities available to workers at the Argyle diamond mine in Western Australia. The motel-style village at the mine site provides self-contained accommodation for 280 mine workers.

A nine-year-old plantation of Macleay poplars at Wauchope,
west of Port Macquarie, in New South Wales. The poplars are to
be used for making matches, veneer, furniture, and mouldings.

Swimming in the rock pool at the southern end of Palm Beach, a
northern Sydney suburb, is a popular pastime among many of
the locals. Located at the tip of the Barrenjoey peninsula, Palm
Beach is one of Sydney's exclusive beaches.

(Below) Saltwater crocodiles lurk in swamp waters on Cape York Peninsula. The saltwater crocodile, which can grow to a length of five metres, inhabits the coastal rivers and swamps of northern and north-eastern Australia.

(Right) Another kind of crocodile, in neon, identifies the Sweethearts Cocktail Bar at the Diamond Beach Hotel Casino in Darwin in the Northern Territory.

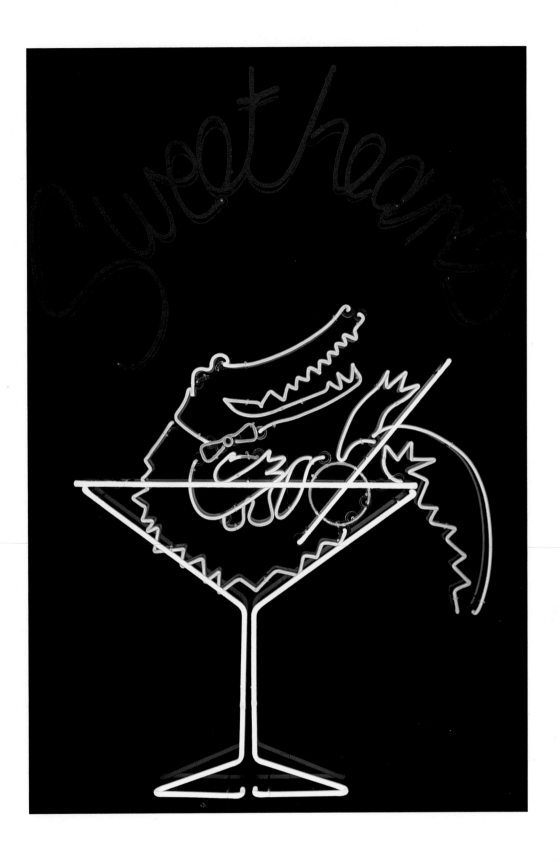

A couple of fishermen share a day at the exclusive London Lakes fishing resort at Bronte Park in central-west Tasmania. London Lakes is a private wild brown trout habitat which was designed and developed solely for the enjoyment of fly fishers.

(Right) Twin boys with a catch of trevally on their summer holidays at Stanley in north-west Tasmania. Established in 1826, Stanley was one of the early settlements in the state.

(Below) A serious amateur fisherman tries his luck from the pier at Stanley. The pier is a popular fishing spot for tourists.

The northern headland of Bondi Beach in Sydney emits a golden glow in the midst of an impending storm.

(Left) Birds in flight at Queenscliff Pier on the north side of Port Phillip Bay, Victoria.

(Below) American tourists record the brilliant blue waterways and tropical islands of the Whitsunday region off the coast of Queensland. The Whitsundays comprises 74 islands, including six island resorts.

(Above) Sunrise in the Blue Mountains, west of Sydney.

(Left) A cold front encroaches over Ben Buckler, the northern headland of Sydney's famous Bondi Beach.

(Left) A green-fingered employee tends the garden of the Defiance flour mill at Toowoomba, the 'garden city' of Queensland, on the Darling Downs.

(Right) A Bondi Nipper prepares for her future role as a lifesaver. The Nipper movement, a junior arm of the Australian Surf Life Saving Association formed in the early 1960s, has 18,000 members throughout Australia, aged between 7 and 13 years.

(Overleaf) The pink glow of dawn bathes the fresh water of Coongie Lake, about 100 kilometres (60 miles) north-west of Innamincka in the remote Sturt's Stony Desert region of South Australia.

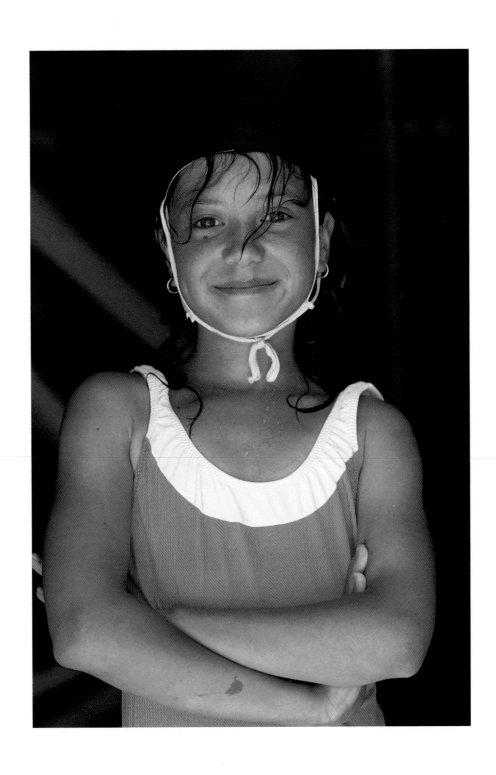

(Above) Windmill at sunset, Deniliquin, New South Wales.

(Right) Chain lightning creates a dramatic effect in the night sky during a freak electrical storm over Sturt's Stony Desert, north-west of Innamincka, in South Australia.

(Overleaf) The Australian Youth Orchestra performs at the Sydney Opera House to celebrate the sponsorship of a grand Bicentennial tour to the United Kingdom and Europe. International touring has taken the orchestra to China, the United States and South-East Asia.

(Right) Harvesting the lavender at Bridestowe lavender farm at Scottsdale in the north-east of Tasmania. The farm is open to the public from December to February.

(Below) The Jackson oilfield in south-west Queensland, one of the largest on-shore oilfields in Australia. Most of the on-shore petroleum exploration in Australia is conducted in Queensland.

(Overleaf) The Sydney Harbour Bridge at dusk. The towering steel-arch span is the most massive in the world.

A milk bar in north-west New South Wales is left deserted after an exodus of young people in search of employment.

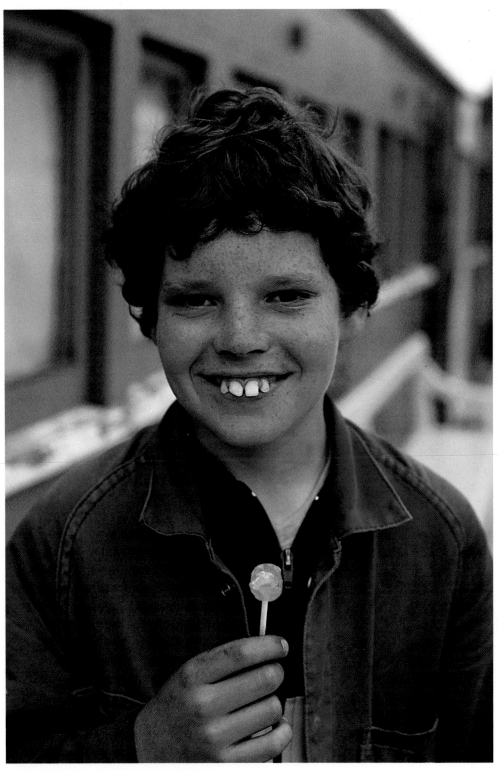

Robert Wilson, a younger-than-average guard on the miniature
train 'Bandicoot' at Deloraine in Tasmania.

Mrs Perry, of the travelling Perry Bros
Circus, in Perth, Western Australia.
The circus was about to embark on its
first tour of the Top End in the
Northern Territory.

Luna Park, on the northern side of Sydney Harbour, at Milsons Point, has retained its popularity as an amusement park for more than 50 years. Founded in 1935, the park was constructed on the staging site used for the building of the Sydney Harbour Bridge. During its refurbishment in 1980, many of the original Art Deco features were preserved, including the famous smiling face at the entrance. Some of the structures are classified by the National Trust.

(Overleaf) A former homestead, now used as a hay shed, stands alone in the Mallee district of north-western Victoria. The Mallee is prime wheat and sheep country.

Sun sails covering the one-kilometre-long site for World Expo '88 give a futuristic flavour to the Queensland capital city of Brisbane. The third largest city in Australia, Brisbane has a population of one million.

129

Sunset at Palm Beach public wharf at Pittwater Park in northern Sydney. The wharf services local ferry trips and tours to the Hawkesbury River.

Black swans gather at dusk on the Coorong, 180 kilometres (110 miles) south of Adelaide in South Australia. The Coorong is a haven for birds, with more than 400 different species to be seen along the shallow and narrow saltwater lagoon.

The sun goes down over the Australian national capital,
Canberra. Designed by the American landscape architect Walter
Burley Griffin, Canberra was founded in 1913.

Melbourne from the inner city suburb of Carlton, at dusk.

(Right) The neon sign of the Sunrise Motel at Queanbeyan, New South Wales, on the Australian Capital Territory border.

(Below) Dusk at Hamilton Island, in the heart of the Great Barrier Reef. This luxurious island resort has its own jet airstrip and a floating marina of more than 200 boats.

(Overleaf) Tourists on a Hamilton Island cruise return sun-burnt and pleasantly tired after a day of scuba diving, swimming and coral viewing on the Great Barrier Reef.

(Above) Low tide during a November sunrise exposes the mudflats at Trinity Bay near Cairns, in northern Queensland. Cairns, a major tourist centre, attracts marlin fishing enthusiasts from all over the world.

(Right) Black clouds at dusk mask a one-way city street in the southern state capital of Hobart, Tasmania.

(Previous page) Sea birds flock around a deserted helipad owned by the Hamilton Island resort in the Whitsunday Passage, Queensland. The helipad is a regular landing spot for visitors to the Great Barrier Reef.

Two young Samoan men exhibit traditional South Sea Island dress at a Pacific Festival at Bondi Beach in Sydney. The main centre at the beach for activities such as festivals, theatre and exhibitions is the Bondi Pavilion, built in 1928.

A Perth newspaper vendor sells copies of the state capital's
afternoon daily tabloid in the standard red regalia.

Members of the Fitzroy Stars Youth Club practise the art of kick boxing at the club gymnasium in Melbourne. Kick boxing, which originated in Thailand, entails a minimum of eight kicks per round.

A young cellist performs for one of the annual Australian concert series given by the Australian Youth Orchestra. The orchestra provides an invaluable training ground for musicians aged from 15 to 23 years.

Employees at the West Footscray plant
of Monsanto Australia in Melbourne
fight a simulated chemical fire on the
premises. Monsanto, a major chemical
company, is unusual in having its own
fire training ground.

(Overleaf) Two men dance the
Zeimpekiko, a traditional Greek dance,
at a Greek engagement party in the
city of Melbourne, Victoria.
Melbourne has more Greek residents
than any city outside Greece.

153

A worker at the Cairns bulk sugar
terminal cleans up the debris. Sugar
is a major export earner for Australia,
with 2.5 million tonnes of sugar
exported each year.

(Above) A group of ladies gather in the Victorian Racing Club members' enclosure at Flemington for Australia's richest horserace, the Melbourne Cup. First held in 1861, the famous Melbourne Cup is one of the main fashion and social events of the year; in Victoria, it is celebrated as a public holiday.

(Right) Party-goers celebrate the Cairns Amateur race meeting, Queensland's answer to the Melbourne Cup.

(Right) Spectators at the Melbourne Cup glimpse a close-up
view of the action at Flemington Racecourse.

(Below) Spectators at a rodeo at Mareeba, west of Cairns. Held
every year in July, the Mareeba Rodeo is known throughout
Australia and attracts top horsemen as well as thousands of visitors.

Ken Connelly, complete with Dallas hat, works his sheep during a dusty late afternoon in the foothills of the Victorian high country at Banambra in the Snowy Mountains. An experienced horseman, Ken was a stuntman in *The Man from Snowy River,* an Australian film classic.

Cattlemen on a mountain ridge in the cool alpine area around Mount Buller in Victoria drive their herds back to the lowlands for grazing at the end of summer.

(Left) A sawmill worker at Smithton, on the north-west coast of Tasmania. The centre of Tasmania's blackwood sawmilling industry, Smithton produces 70 to 80 per cent of Australia's blackwood timber.

(Right) Gladys Woolley, proud mother of 12 and grandmother of 32, demonstrates traditional country hospitality with a jug of lime cordial at home at Glenhuon, 50 kilometres (31 miles) south-west of Hobart.

(Right) Kids make their own entertainment on the roadside in a tiny seaside town near Port Arthur in Tasmania.

(Below) The Playford Street Pals perform in front of the town mayor in Mount Gambier, South Australia.

(Above) Merino sheep are rounded up for shearing at a stud property at Deniliquin in south-west New South Wales.

(Left) Local woolbuyer Max Poulton shows off a sample of the quality fleece at his produce store in Mudgee in the Golden West district of New South Wales. Mudgee is a major sheep and wheat area, also famous for its honey and fine wines.

Operators engage in frantic trading on the floor of the Sydney Stock Exchange on 'Black Tuesday', 20 October 1987. Following the biggest world-wide crash since the Great Depression the All Ordinaries Index fell by about 25 per cent.

A crowded late afternoon on Bondi Beach in Sydney.

Mid-afternoon at the saltwater baths in Newcastle,
north of Sydney. The pump-operated baths
opened to the public in 1914.

(Above) A member of the Royal Volunteer Coastal Patrol keeps a watchful eye over the spectator craft outside Sydney Heads at the start of the Sydney-to-Hobart yacht race. The race, which begins on Boxing Day each year, attracts a huge crowd.

(Right) A bather at Wiley's Baths, otherwise known as the 'sun strip', one of three rock pools at the south end of Coogee Beach, one of Sydney's southern beaches.

(Right) Local fishermen haul in an early morning catch at Sandon Bluffs, near Grafton, in northern New South Wales.

(Below) An elderly couple take a stroll along a secluded beach at Apollo Bay in Victoria.

A rainbow adds a colourful glow to a pastoral scene in the
Orange district of New South Wales. Located on the Central
Tablelands, west of Sydney, Orange is a major centre for mixed
farming and the growing of stone fruits.

A wild dingo makes an appearance on a deserted beach on
Fraser Island, 11 kilometres (seven miles) off the southern coast
of Queensland. Dingoes, which belong to the same species as
the domestic dog, are found throughout mainland Australia.

A local cafe caters for a variety of tastes at Rainbow Beach on the southern Queensland coast. Rainbow Beach is famous for its coloured sands.

(Right) A noisy flock of corellas, members of the cockatoo family, take refuge in a eucalypt tree in the Northern Territory. The birds find hollows in the eucalypts for nesting.

(Below) The vast Flinders Ranges National Park in South Australia covers 78,500 hectares (193,895 acres), extending about 40 kilometres (25 miles) north of Wilpena. The park, formerly a sheep station, is a haven for red kangaroos, euros, emus, galahs, corellas and wedge-tailed eagles.

(Overleaf) A surf carnival draws a large crowd at Freshwater Beach north of Sydney. The first surf carnival was held at Manly in 1908, two years after the founding of Australia's first surf lifesaving club at Bondi.

(Previous page) Alexandria cattle station, in the Barkly Tableland, Northern Territory. The station covers a vast area of 8,391 square kilometres (3,240 square miles).

(Left) Thousands of City to Surf competitors make an eager start in the annual race from William Street in Sydney to Bondi Beach. The 14 kilometre (8.4-mile) race, which attracts up to 30,000 participants, is held in the second week of August.

(Above) Festive flags decorate a Perth city street during the finals of the 1987 America's Cup, in Western Australia.

(Left) Guests recline by the pool on the rooftop of the Perth International Hotel in Western Australia. The Perth International is one of seven five-star hotels in the state's capital.

Aboriginal women from the Bardi tribe gather shells for jewellery making on the reef at the One Arm Point Aboriginal reserve in Western Australia.

A baby is left temporarily unattended during a dog-training session in the well-to-do suburb of Heidelberg in Melbourne. The Saturday afternoon obedience-training classes are conducted by the Kintala Club.

A throng of fashion-parade spectators lunch in the shade of a
marquee at a Woollahra mansion in Sydney's eastern suburbs.

(Right) An immaculate garden in full bloom greets the local postman on his daily rounds during the annual Carnival of Flowers in Toowoomba on Queensland's Darling Downs. The carnival, which is held throughout September, attracts thousands of admirers every year.

(Below) Refreshments are served in the garden by a proud exhibitor in the Toowoomba Carnival of Flowers. Local residents open their gardens to the public every spring for competition and charity.

A gardener tends a miniature Tudor village in the Fitzroy Gardens in East Melbourne. Built by Edgar Wilson, a pensioner from Norwood in England, the village was presented to the City of Melbourne by the London borough of Lambeth in May 1948 in appreciation of Melbourne's generosity in sending food to Britain during the Second World War.

(Above) An empty track at the QEII Jubilee Sports Centre in Brisbane. The QEII, which opened in 1979, was the site for the athletics events of the 1982 Commonwealth Games.

(Right) Nobel Prize-winning Australian author Patrick White joins a protest against the Sydney monorail outside the Town Hall, in George Street, Sydney.

(Above) Aboriginal children at play at the Tea Tree Primary School, 180 kilometres (112 miles) north of Alice Springs, in the Northern Territory. The small town of Tea Tree, which is surrounded by Aboriginal and white pastoral stations, was a staging post for Australian military convoys on their way to Darwin during the Second World War.

(Right) A young cotton farm worker leaves the irrigation site of a 10,000-hectare (25,000-acre) commercial farm at Warren, in north-west New South Wales. Warren is a major cotton-growing area, also famous for its merino wool.

(Above) Passengers on the Indian-Pacific transcontinental train crossing the Nullarbor Plain in Western Australia. The 4,800-kilometre (3,000 mile) journey from Sydney to Perth, takes three nights and two days.

(Left) Maree Whiteley experiences the nostalga of a steam train ride on the Don River Railway at Deloraine in Tasmania.

(Above) Red Rock lookout in Victoria. The view from the rock takes in 50 to 60 lakes around the township of Colac, which stands on the edge of the world's largest volcanic plain.

(Left) The view across the Nullarbor Plain from the Indian-Pacific train in Western Australia.

(Overleaf) Camels in training for the Great Camel Race from Uluru in the centre of the continent to Queensland's Gold Coast – a special event for the 1988 Australian Bicentenary.
The camels and converted kombi-van, sighted here on the Oodnadatta Track, north of William Creek in northern South Australia, had been on the road for four months.

(Above) Advertising, Queensland style — an arresting image is displayed in the front yard of a house at Cairns.

(Right) A regular Australian truckie stops for a meal break at Gundagai in the Southern Tablelands of New South Wales.

(Overleaf) A chimney stack casts a trail of smoke over a Mount Isa mine site in far western Queensland. Mount Isa, the most extensive city in the world, covers an area of nearly 41,000 square kilometres (24,600 square miles), which is twice the size of Israel. The Mount Isa mine is the world's largest single producer of silver and lead.

(Above) The face of a shearer at White Cliffs, in the far north-west of New South Wales. White Cliffs is a solar-powered town, more commonly known for its opal mining.

(Left) Bev and Tom, owners of the 'Funny Farm', an animal farm at Port Arthur in Tasmania. Port Arthur, on the Tasman Peninsula, near Hobart, is the site of an infamous penal settlement.

The Great Victoria Desert, in the south-eastern part of Western Australia, has parallel sand dunes running east-west and is one of the most uninhabited parts of the continent.

A flock of galahs fly over wheat stubble in the Mallee in north-
west Victoria. Galahs, the most populous of all the cockatoos,
are common throughout Australia.

(Left) A weather-worn station hand reclines against his vehicle at Rosella Plains cattle station in north-west Queensland. The region's savanna country is suited to extensive grazing.

(Overleaf) An historic woolshed built out of the local rock at Cordillo Downs, a sheep station in Sturt's Stony Desert in north-east South Australia.

(Left) A sun-bronzed labourer soaks up the sun while working on the construction of a bridge across a dry river bed at Karratha in north-west Western Australia.

(Right) Sawmill worker Brian ('Corky') Fletcher spares a moment for the camera during a day at Duncan's sawmill at Eden in New South Wales. A quiet and charming fishing port located 48 kilometres (30 miles) from the New South Wales-Victorian border, Eden was once the centre of a thriving whaling industry.

(Left) More than 20,000 Aborigines from all over the country respond to the 1988 Bicentennial celebrations with a mass demonstration in Sydney on Australia Day. Aborigines constitute 1.5 per cent of the population of Australia.

(Above right) An Aboriginal plays traditional tribal music at a ceremony at Uluru (Ayers Rock) in the Northern Territory.

(Below right) A ceremony to commemorate the handing over of Uluru to the Uluru Katatjuta Aboriginal Land Trust, which holds the title on behalf of the Pitjantjatjara and Yankunytjatjara peoples, by the Australian government in October 1985.

(Above) The New South Wales Fire Brigade band parades at the 1986 Rugby League grand final at the Sydney Cricket Ground. The 30-minute parade, comprising a range of spectacular events, is traditionally held before the main game.

(Left) Members of the Melbourne Metropolian Fire Brigade participate in fire drill at the MFB's headquarters in Albert Street, East Melbourne. The drill was being performed in preparation for a visit from the Victorian Governor.

(Left) Walls of glass create a series of interesting mirror images at a construction site in the commercial heart of the garden city of Canberra in the Australian Capital Territory.

(Right) An engineer perches on one of the steel girders of the Argyle diamond mine site, 200 kilometres (125 miles) south of Kununurra in the Kimberley region of Western Australia. Argyle is Australia's only commercial diamond mine.

(Left) A commuter strolls down to Victoria's Queenscliff Pier during a late afternoon in autumn. Regular hydrofoil services to Portsea and Melbourne are conducted across Port Phillip Bay.

(Overleaf) Glendarra sheep station in the north-west region of New South Wales, near Broken Hill. The area is a major merino wool-growing area, with properties like this one running about 6,000 sheep on almost 26,000 hectares (64,000 acres).

(Above) A station hand sorts cattle in the yards at Spring Creek in the dry north-western region of Queensland.

(Right) A stray steer which has been lassoed, is carted by truck to the cattle yards during mustering at Rosella Plains cattle station in north-west Queensland.

(Above) Young ballet students practise the finer points of
classical dance at the Karen Stephens Academy of Dance at
Prahran in Melbourne. The academy is a private school catering
for all ages over four years.

(Right) Ami M'Bodj, a seven-year-old ballet student at the Karen
Stephens Academy.

A worker emerges from the top of the Sydney Harbour Bridge.
The bridge, which opened on 19 March 1932, took nine years
to build and is 134 metres (440 feet) high from mean sea level
to the top of the arch.

Scrap metal is gathered for recycling at the Holden's Motor Company manufacturing plant at Dandenong in Victoria. Holden's is the largest automotive exporter in Australia.

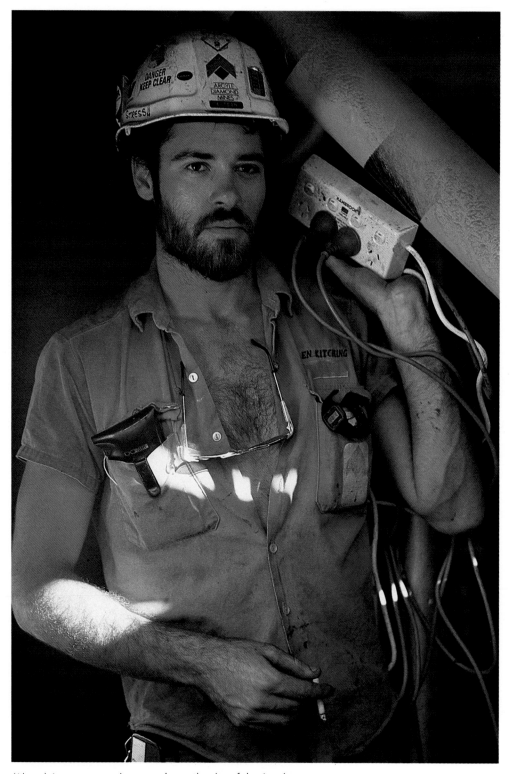

(Above) A contract engineer works on the site of the Argyle diamond mine in Western Australia. Argyle produces more diamonds than any other mine in the world — 30 million carats of diamonds a year.

(Right) The wharf at Port Hedland, Western Australia, is hosed down in preparation for the shipping of ore from the Mount Newman mine, 400 kilometres (250 miles) away by rail.

(Left) The Railway Hotel at Coolgardie in Western Australia, the scene in the 1890s of one of the biggest gold rushes in Australian history. The road has been covered in red sand for a location shot in the Australian film *Boundaries of the Heart*.

(Below) Country mailboxes on the roadside at Yass, a wealthy wool-growing area in the south of New South Wales.

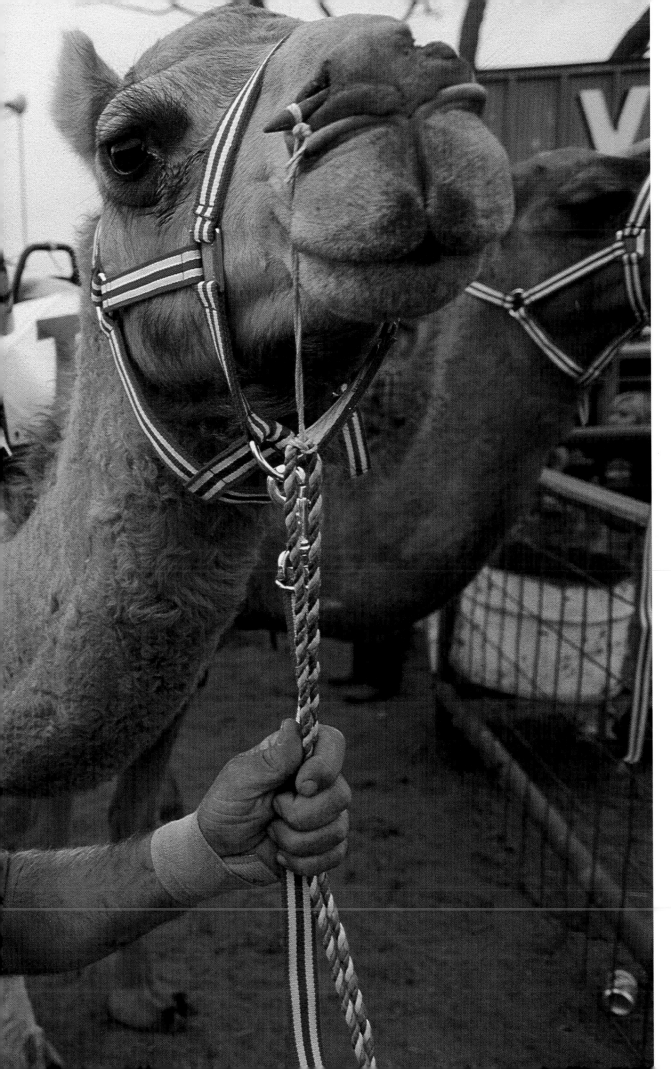

Camel trainer Noel Fullerton prepares one of his animals for a race on a farm near Alice Springs in the Northern Territory. Camel races are a popular attraction in the Territory.

247

(Above) A tomato picker at Carnarvon in the Gascoyne region of Western Australia. The centre supplies the southern part of the state with fresh fruit and vegetables all year round.

(Right) A caravan park attendant engages in his daily rounds at the Yulara Resort in the Northern Territory. The resort, which includes a five-star hotel, is near the Uluru National Park.

A Mount Newman miner enjoys a game of golf on a red-earth
fairway in the Hamersley Ranges in Western Australia.

Boxing kangaroos near Tidbinbilla Mountain in the Australian Capital Territory.

A family at home in their dug-out at Coober Pedy, a major opal-mining town in central South Australia. Many of the locals live in dug-outs — houses that have been dug into the sides of the hills to provide protection from the extreme temperatures.

Pat Leslie, a local crayfisherman, at home with the family at
Couta Rocks, near Temma in north-west Tasmania.

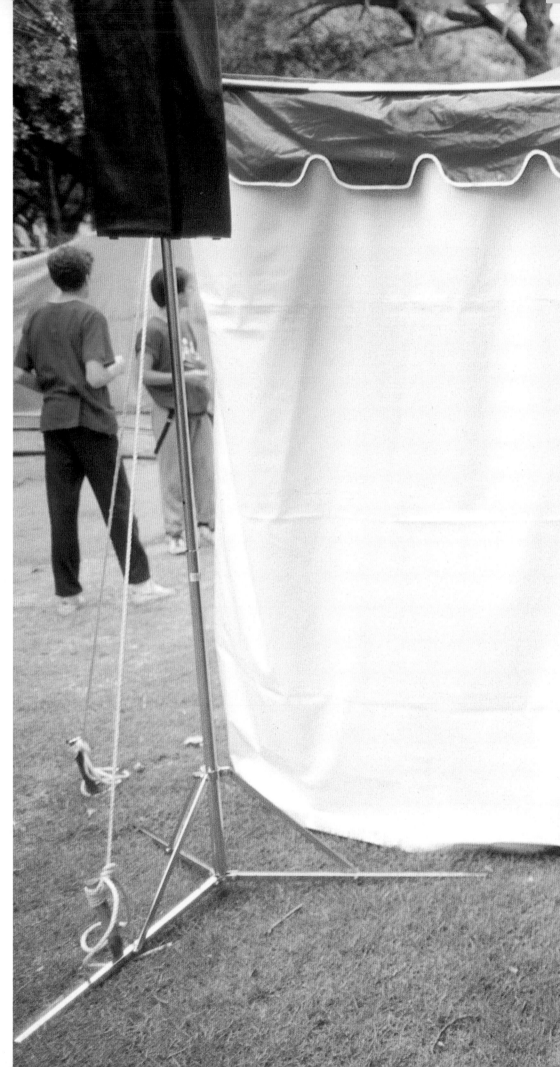

(Above) Two young sisters busk in Hyde Park during the annual Festival of Sydney. The January festival is a celebration combining art, theatre, music and free public events.

(Right) A young musician warms up behind the scenes for the Carols by Candlelight annual Christmas concert at the Domain in Sydney. The free open-air concert, a popular family event, attracts thousands of spectators every year.

(Right) Members of a group of 1,500 Scouts from all over New South Wales contribute to the festivities of the Rugby League 'Grand Final Spectacular' at the Sydney Cricket Ground.

(Left) One of a team of private parachutists descends on the Sydney Cricket Ground – a visual highlight of the annual Rugby League 'Grand Final Spectacular'.

(Below) A police helicopter lands at Sorrento on Port Phillip Bay near Melbourne. The Victorian police operate three helicopters for air search and rescue purposes.

The Parramatta team celebrates its victory over Canterbury-Bankstown in the 1986 Rugby League grand final at the Sydney Cricket Ground.

Torres Strait Islanders wear traditional
dress for a celebratory feast at Bamaga
on Cape York in Queensland.

(Left) Three-year-old Simone Clark pauses outside the bluestone general store at Lake Bolac in the western district of Victoria. Western Victoria is a wealthy sheep and wheat area.

(Right) The popular Swanettes raise a cheer for the Australian Rules team, the Sydney Swans, at the Sydney Cricket Ground. During the playing season, from April to September, the Swans drew crowds at the SCG of up to 40,000.

(Left) Briony Prider, a member of the Playford Street Pals, performs in a backyard concert in Mount Gambier, South Australia. The group of 14 children aged between 7 and 14 years raises money for the support of a Javanese child through World Vision.

(Right) The face of a happy tourist on Hamilton Island in Queensland.

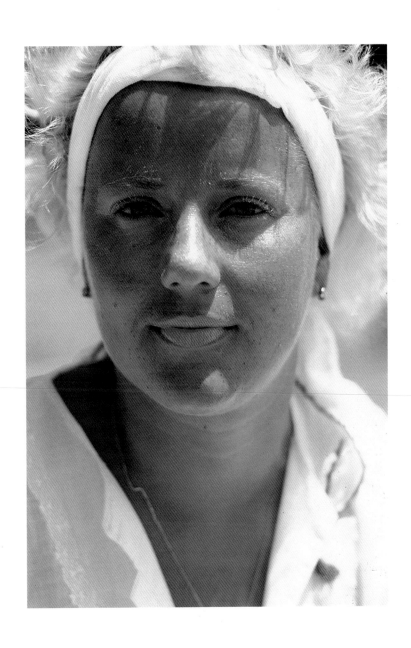

Young members of the North Bondi and Elouera surf clubs compete in a surf carnival at Bondi Beach in Sydney. The Surf Life Saving Association, which was established in 1907, comprises 247 clubs throughout Australia with a total of more than 60,000 members aged from seven years.

Kids sample some of the water-based activities at the
Adventure World theme park in the Perth suburb of Kardinya.
Activities such as these reflect the Perth summer lifestyle.

Riding 'The Bush Beast' — the biggest roller-coaster in the Southern Hemisphere — at Australia's Wonderland, at Eastern Creek, west of Sydney. The roller-coaster, which is constructed of southern yellow pine, is 27.5 metres (90 feet) high, the equivalent of nine storeys.

Two friends in the heart of Kimberley cattle country at Fitzroy Crossing in Western Australia. Cattle were brought overland from Queensland and New South Wales around the turn of the century in drives that were longer than the famous Colorado and Arizona trails in North America.

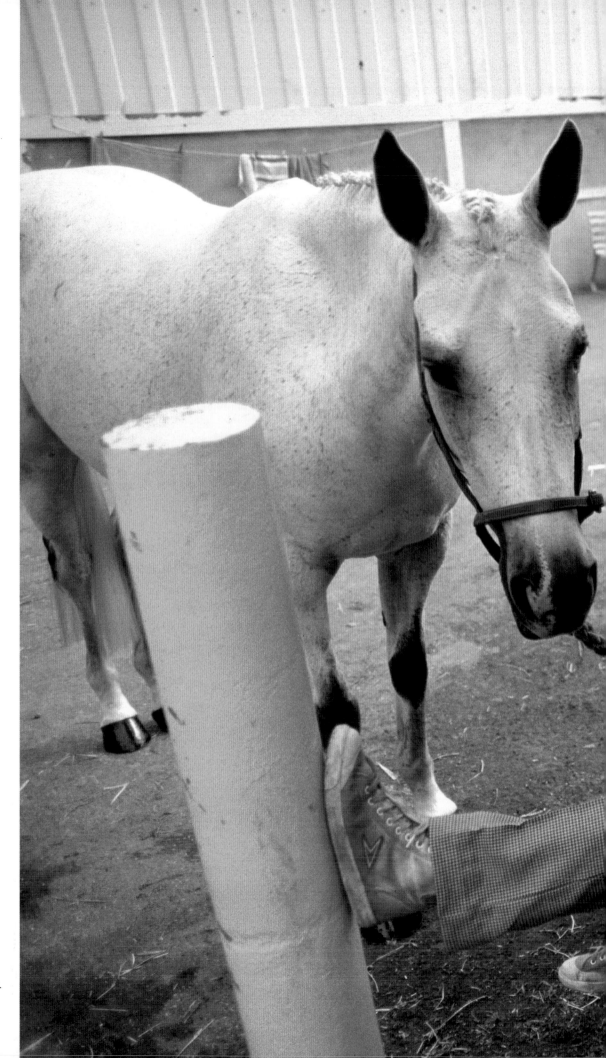

A boy and his horse relax behind the scenes at the Royal Easter Show in Sydney. The show, run by the Royal Agricultural Society of New South Wales, attracts a million visitors a year.

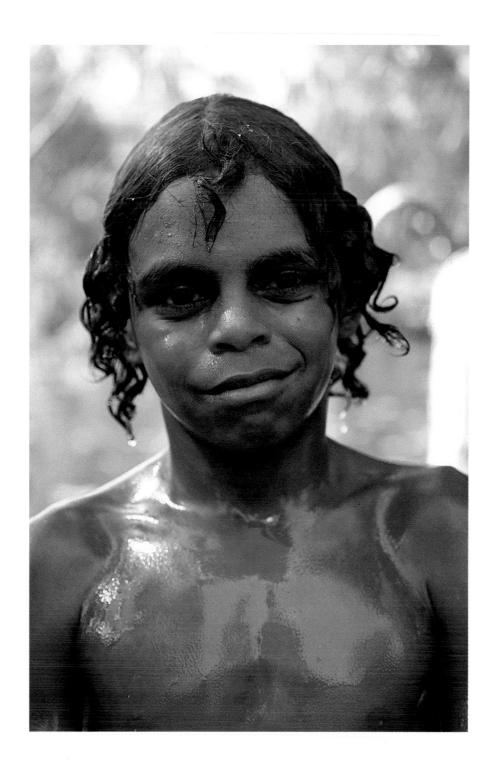

(Left) A young Torres Strait Islander emerges after a swim in the river at Bamaga on Cape York Peninsula. Bamaga is one of the three Islander settlements on the tip of the peninsula.

(Below) Torres Strait Islander children dry off after a swim in the river at Bamaga.

(Right) Schoolgirls give a lunch-time concert to raise money for charity in Hobart City Square in Tasmania.

(Below) A group of primary school children learn about road safety while developing their bicycle-riding skills as part of an education program run by the South-East Queensland Driver Education Centre in Gympie, Queensland.

(Below) A super-cart, a type of motorised go-cart, burns around the track at the Calder Park Raceway in Melbourne. The powerful vehicles reach speeds of up to 240 kilometres (150 miles) per hour.

(Right) Cleaners board an Ansett jet in Melbourne between flights. Ansett has a huge fleet of modern aircraft, which serve all the capital cities throughout Australia.

(Below) Waiting for the bus at Bowral, a country retreat in the Southern Highlands in New South Wales.

(Overleaf) This unusual sculptural formation of boulders, known as Remarkable Rocks, is a well-known landmark on the south-west end of Kangaroo Island, off the coast of South Australia.

(Above) The view looking east over the Pacific Ocean from the
Sydney suburb of Dover Heights.

(Right) A shipping beacon reflects the afternoon light at Barwon Heads, 20 kilometres (13 miles) from Geelong, in Victoria.

(Overleaf) Sunset at Ocean Grove Beach, on the Bellarine Peninsula in Victoria. The fashionable family holiday beach is popular with day trippers from Melbourne and Geelong.

A plane comes in for an emergency landing at Barkly Downs
cattle station on the Barkly Tableland in western Queensland.

A sugarcane farmer near Cairns, in northern Queensland, burns off his crop before harvesting. Most of the sugar exported by Australia goes to Canada, Japan, South Korea, Malaysia, Singapore and New Zealand.

THE PHOTOGRAPHERS

Each photographer is represented on the following pages:

GRENVILLE TURNER
Pages *2-3, *4-5, *14-15, *26-27, *28-29, *30-31, *38-39, *42-43, 46, 57, 65, *66-67, 69, *74-75, 82-83, *86-87, *110-111, *113, 114-115, *118-119, 122-123, *124 (Below), 145, 148-149, *160-161, 168, *178-179, *184, *188-189, 192, 193, *210-211, *214-215, *217, *222-223, *225, 234-235, 240, *249, 252, 267, *270-271, 278-279, *284, Back Cover.

CAROLYN JOHNS
Pages 49, 51, 52-53, 56, 70, 76, 77, 80, 81, 84, 93, *95, 98-99, 100, 101, *104, 105, 117, 121, *130-131, 136, 138-139, 140-141, 143, *144, 164, 165, 167, *190-191, 194-195, *198-199, *204, 206, 216, 231, *232-233, 242, 243, *244, 250, 253, *262, 265, *266, 269, 274 (Above), *282-283, *288.

PHILIP QUIRK
Front Cover, Pages 1, *17, *18-19, 25, *32-33, *34, *35, *36, *37, *40, *41, *44-45, *54-55, *58-59, *61, *64, *73, *78-79, *88-89, *90-91, *92, *97, *102-103, *106, *107, 108, 112, *116, *124 (Top), *125, *126-127, *128-129, *133, *134-135, *137, 142, 146-147, *150-151, 152-153, 154-155, 156, 157, 158, *159, *162-163, 169, *172-173, *174-175, 176, *180, *185, *186-187, 196-197, 200-201, *202, *203, 212 (Left), *219, 220-221, *227 (Above & Below), *228, *229 *236, *237, 238, 239, 241, *245, *246-247, *251, *254, 255, 256 (Below), *268, 275, *276, 277, *280, *281, 285.

OLIVER STREWE
Pages *16, *20-21, *22-23, *24, 47, 48, *50, *60, 62, 63, 68, *71, *72, *85, *94, *96, *109, *120, 132, 166, *170-171 *177, 178 (Left), 181, 182-183, *205, 207, 208, 209, 213, *218, 224, *226, *230, 248, 256 (Above), 257, 258-259, 260-261, 263, 264, 272, 273, 274 (Below).

*Denotes copyright ownership by photographer.
All other photographs dual copyright Wildlight/Soundsense.

GRENVILLE TURNER

Grenville Turner's experience in commercial photography dates from the late 1960s when he arrived in Sydney from England.

His images reflect a fascination with the physical realities of heat, light and distance in the Australian environment, and the effects of these elements on its people.

The work shown at his 1987 exhibition *Horizons* (Festival Theatre, Adelaide) provides extensive documentation of the Strzelecki and Simpson Deserts, Lake Eyre, Cooper Creek and the Flinders Ranges.

He has published two books: *Akubra is Australian for Hat,* a collection of images of the ubiquitous Aussie bush hat; and *Australian Forestry and its People,* a reflection of his keen interest in conservation.

Grenville Turner has been an associate photographer at Wildlight since its creation.

CAROLYN JOHNS

After ten years of nursing, Carolyn Johns studied photodocumentation with *Magnum* photographers in Europe, where she later freelanced as a photojournalist.

Returning to Melbourne in 1981 she specialised in portraiture, a social document- ation depicting both the ordinary working Australian and celebrities from the world of film-making.

Johns has been the stills photographer for major feature films, including *Mad Max II, Warm Nights on a Slow Moving Train* and *Boundaries of the Heart.*

She has photographed many celebrities at work, including Bob Dylan, Linda Evans, Mel Gibson, Barry Humphries and New Zealand PM David Lange.

Johns has also worked on commissioned photographic assignments for *Traveler, Time* and the London *Observer.*

Book assignments have included *A Day in the Life of Australia, A Day in the Life of New South Wales, Sex in Australia* and *Nursing for Life.*

PHILIP QUIRK

Philip Quirk, a founding member of Wildlight, has exhibited widely throughout the world.

His work is represented by Macquarie Galleries in Sydney and in public galleries, including the Australian National Gallery, the Phillip Morris Trust and the Parliament House collection in Canberra, and the Art Gallery of New South Wales in Sydney.

Quirk's work provides a multi-faceted documentation of life in Australia.

His work is included in numerous local and international publications, such as *National Geographic, Geo* Germany, *Geo* Australia and *Time Australia.*

Books he has worked on include *A Day in the Life of Australia, A Salute to Singapore,* and *On the Beach.*

He has also contributed to annual reports of corporations such as Shell Australia.

OLIVER STREWE

Oliver Strewe has worked on many assignments for overseas and Australian publications, including the *New York Times* colour magazine, *National Geographic, Australian Geographic, Observer* magazine (London), *Sunday Times, Newsweek* and *Time.*

Book publications include *Bondi* (James Fraser, 1984) and *The Workers,* with text by Blanche d'Alpuget (William Collins, 1987).

Strewe has covered such significant events as the Portuguese withdrawal from East Timor and the celebrations for independence of New Guinea, the Solomon Islands and Vanuatu.

He has exhibited widely in Australia and England. His *Death Before Dishonour* portfolio, a collection of images of tattoos, was purchased by the National Library in Canberra. Strewe concentrates on depicting the Australian people and their landscape. Many of his images have been used on the covers of *Time* and Australian *Geo.*

Oliver Strewe is a founding member of Wildlight.

The glittering grand finale of the biggest fireworks display ever
held in Australia explodes over Sydney Harbour Bridge on
Australia Day 1988, celebrating 200 years of white settlement.